INTERNET GLOSSARY

INTERNET GLOSSARY

B.G. KUTAIS (EDITOR)

Novinka Books
New York

Senior Editors: Susan Boriotti and Donna Dennis
Coordinating Editor: Tatiana Shohov
Office Manager: Annette Hellinger
Graphics: Wanda Serrano
Editorial Production: Jennifer Vogt, Matthew Kozlowski and Maya Columbus
Circulation: Ave Maria Gonzalez, Indah Becker, Raymond Davis and Vladimir Klestov
Communications and Acquisitions: Serge P. Shohov
Marketing: Cathy DeGregory

Library of Congress Cataloging-in-Publication Data
Available Upon Request

ISBN: 1-59033-297-0.

Copyright © 2002 by Novinka Books
An Imprint of Nova Science Publishers, Inc.
400 Oser Ave, Suite 1600
Hauppauge, New York 11788-3619
Tele. 631-231-7269   Fax 631-231-8175
e-mail: Novascience@earthlink.net
Web Site: http://www.novapubishers.com

All rights reserved. No part of this book may be reproduced, stored in a retrieval system or transmitted in any form or by any means: electronic, electrostatic, magnetic, tape, mechanical photocopying, recording or otherwise without permission from the publishers.

The authors and publisher have taken care in preparation of this book, but make no expressed or implied warranty of any kind and assume no responsibility for any errors or omissions. No liability is assumed for incidental or consequential damages in connection with or arising out of information contained in this book.

This publication is designed to provide accurate and authoritative information with regard to the subject matter covered herein. It is sold with the clear understanding that the publisher is not engaged in rendering legal or any other professional services. If legal or any other expert assistance is required, the services of a competent person should be sought. FROM A DECLARATION OF PARTICIPANTS JOINTLY ADOPTED BY A COMMITTEE OF THE AMERICAN BAR ASSOCIATION AND A COMMITTEE OF PUBLISHERS.

Printed in the United States of America

CONTENTS

Preface vii

Glossary 1

Index 53

PREFACE

Hundreds of millions of people search the Internet every day throughout the world. In the process, they are exposed to the ever-confusing jargon, which envelops it: ISPs, protocols, search engines etc. Yet few have the foggiest clue what the words mean. This glossary presents the words of the Net and their meanings along with introductory articles explaining searching as well as indexes reaching deeper into the terms and their meanings.

GLOSSARY

Access provider: 1. An organization that provides users with access to a computer network. **2.** A party responsible for traffic originating and terminating in jurisdictional areas defined by regulatory agencies.

Access: 1. The ability and means necessary to store data in, to retrieve data from, to communicate with, or to make use of any resource of a system. **2.** To obtain the use of a resource. **3.** (COMSEC) [The] capability and opportunity to gain detailed knowledge of or to alter information or material. [NIS] **4.** (AIS) [The] ability and means to communicate with (*i.e.*, input to or receive output from), or otherwise make use of any information, resource, or component in an AIS. *Note [for 3 and 4]:* An individual does not have "access" if the proper authority or a physical, technical, or procedural measure prevents him/her from obtaining knowledge or having an opportunity to alter information, material, resources, or components. [NIS] **5.** An assigned portion of system resources for one data stream of user communications or signaling. **6.** [An] opportunity to make use of an information-system (IS) resource.

Address: A unique number or name that identifies a specific computer or user on a network.

AFAIK: Acronym for As Far As I Know, sometimes encountered in E-mail or usenet news postings.

ALL-IN-1: Character cell menu-based software that users of OUVAXA (primarily employees) interact with for E-mail and internet access.

Alternate access provider: A company that enters a market area as a competitive service provider (CAP) to provide exchange service in competition with one or more existing exchange carrier (s) in the same market area.

AppleTalk: The protocols used by networks of Macintosh computers and their printers. See also LocalTalk, EtherTalk and TCP/IP.

Application: A software program that performs a particular, useful function for you. Examples include WordPerfect, VersaTerm, EXCEL, etc.

Application: a computer program, which performs a set of tasks forming a defined function or service.

Archie: A system used to search for files that are publicly available by anonymous FTP. See also, Veronica. Further definition: Software that creates and searches an index of the names and locations of files that are available for file transfer through the Internet.

Archive: An FTP host; a file (typically compressed) that contains multiple other files.

ASCII: Acronym for American Standard Code for Information Interchange; pronounced "askee." On most computer systems, except IBM mainframes, ASCII is the standard way to represent letters and punctuation marks with numbers. Often used as an adjective to describe text files. A standard used to encode data into a machine-readable format that is used for transmitting text.

Attachment: In e-mail, a computer file that is transmitted with an e-mail message. *Note:* Attachments are converted by an e-mail manager program, or by an add-on, to a MIME (multipurpose Internet mail extension) or binary format. The files are recovered by the recipient's e-mail manager program or by an add-on into their original, usually application-specific, format.

Authentication: a mechanism of using information resources to verify the claimed identity of a party to a transaction or an entity involved in a transaction.

Authorisation: an authentication process whereby predetermined rights, including access to information resources, are granted to users or entities

AXP: High performance, general purpose host computer system manufactured by Digital Equipment Corporation; also known as "Alpha." OAK and OUVAXA are AXP systems.

Backbone: A network that is used to tie several other networks together. A high speed telecommunications network that connects together other slower and smaller computer networks.

Backup file: A copy of a file made for purposes of later reconstruction of the file, if necessary. *Note:* A backup file may be used for preserving the integrity of the original file and may be recorded on any suitable medium.

Backup: 1. [A] copy of files and programs made to facilitate recovery, if necessary.

Bandwidth: Measure of the capacity of a communications channel, expressed in bits per second The rate at which data can be transferred, usually measured in bits per second; often used as a synonym for "throughput." Analogous to "cross-section size" of a water main.

Baud: The number of times per second that a modem changes the signal it transmits. **Only** for the oldest modems (whose signals can be in exactly two states) is this a synonym for the data transmission speed of the modem, in bits per second.

BBS (Bulletin Board System): Dial-up or Telnet-accessible computer systems that use special software to provide access to repositories of messages and files. BBSs are typically managed by individuals.

Bitmap: In computer graphics, a representation of an image (which category includes characters) by code or a codingError! Bookmark not defined. scheme that defines (a) the position of pixels by row (horizontal position) and column (vertical position), and (b) individual pixel characteristics such as gray scale and color. *Loosely synonymous with* **raster.**

BITNET (Because It's Time Network): An academically-oriented network composed of educational and research oriented institutions connected to the Internet, which is intended for the noncommercial distribution of information. Uses the RSCS protocol originally designed for IBM mainframes, not using TCP/IP, and therefore not part of the internet. BITNET has been phased out in favor of the internet.

Bluetooth: A low-power, short-range, rf technology that allows the connection of intelligent communications devices or appliances in a household or an office in a short-range wireless network. Examples of Bluetooth applications are transferring data between cell phones, radios, pagers, personal digital assistants, notebook computers, video and still cameras, audio players, and local area networks.

Bookmark: A name or address of an Internet resource, stored in a software file at a user's site, *e.g.*, in a desktop computer, for convenient future use. *Note:* An example of a bookmark is an entry in a bookmark file (or bookmark list) such as maintained within or by a Web browser for the convenience of the user in revisiting a previously visited Web site.

Bootup: In computer science, the initial sequence of events (usually preprogrammed in firmware present in the computer) that are necessary to start a computer; *i.e.*, to initialize its operating system, load programs into memory, *etc.*, when (a) it is first powered up, or (b) when already powered up, upon some kind of assenting action by the user.

Bridge: A device connecting two similar networks, such as two LANs. See also, Gateway and Router.

Broadband: this transmission medium allows transmission of voice, data and video simultaneously at higher transfer rates. Broadband transmission media generally can carry multiple channels.

Browser: Client software for accessing information provided by servers used to fetch/read documents from the Web, display them on-screen and print them, jump to others via hypertext, view images and listen to audio files. May display that information as plain text or in a graphical format.*Note 1:* Browsers are usually associated with the Internet and the World Wide Web (WWW). *Note 2:* A browser may be able to access information in many formats, and through different services including HTTP and FTP.

Browsing: [The] act of searching through information-system (IS) storage to locate or acquire information without necessarily knowing of the existence or the format of the information being sought.

BTW: Acronym for By The Way, sometimes encountered in E-mail or usenet news postings.

Byte (B): A sequence of contiguous bits (usually 8) considered as a unit. *Note:* In pre-1970 literature, *"byte"* referred to a variable-length bit string. Since that time, the usage has changed so that now it almost always refers to an 8-bit string. This usage predominates in computer and data transmission literature; when so used, the term is synonymous with *" octet."*

Cable modem: In CATV systems, a bidirectional high-speed digital communications interface, located on a subscriber's or user's premises, and used, for example, for Internet access or other digital communications.

ccTLD: country code Top Level Domain refers to a high level Internet Protocol address to identify a country e.g, za for South Africa.

Certificate: a certificate is a public key that has been digitally signed by a trusted authority to identify the user of the public key. SET uses certificates to encrypt for example payment information.

Certification Authority: a secure third party organisation or company that issues digital certificates used to create digital signatures and public key pairs. Certificate authorities guarantee that the two parties exchanging information are really who they claim to be.

CGI: Acronym for Common Gateway Interface, a standard method for having Web pages cause the execution of computer programs on the server. These are routinely used to support Web "forms": pages that provide for the user to enter information. Search engines are examples of CGI-based Web applications.

Click wrap contracts: Contracts concluded in an online environment, usually the Internet, where the terms of a contract are set out and "offered" by one party on a website and the other party indicates "acceptance" of those terms by for example clicking on an "accept" button or icon and hence concluding the contract.

Client: A software component, running on one computer, that accomplishes its tasks by exchanging data and messages with a "server" component running on the same or another computer. Examples include news readers, web and gopher browsers, FTP, and TELNET software.

Client: The computer or software that requests services from another computer or program known as a server.

Coax: (Pronounced as two words, "ko-ax".) Abbreviation of co-axial cable. Wire for data transmission that uses a central conductor surrounded by a layer of insulation, an outer conductor, and a final layer of insulation. Coaxial cable is used for a range of devices, including many ethernet networks and cable TV.

Computer graphics: 1. Graphics implemented through the use of computers. **2.** Methods and techniques for converting data to or from graphic displays via computers. **3.** The branch of science and technology concerned with methods and techniques for converting data to or from visual presentation using computers.

Computer network: 1. A network of data processing nodes that are interconnected for the purpose of data communications. **2.** A communications network in which the end instruments are computers.

Confidentiality: reasonable assurance that online or stored data cannot be viewed and interpreted by any person other than an authorised one.

Connectivity: The capability to provide, to end users, connections to the Internet or other communications networks.

Copyright: the right to retain or sell the rights to an artistic work. Copyright is a form protection to the authors or "original works of authorship" including literary, dramatic, musical, artistic, and certain other intellectual works.

CPU: *Abbreviation for* **central processing unit. 1.** The portion of a computer that includes circuits controlling the interpretation and execution of instructions. **2.** The portion of a computer that executes programmed instructions, performs arithmetic and logical operations on data, and controls input / output functions. *Synonym* **central processor. 3.** *Abbreviation for* **communications processor unit.** A computer embedded in a communications system, *i.e.,* the portion of a digital communications switch that executes programmed instructions, performs arithmetic and logical operations on signals, and controls input/output functions.

Cryptography: practice of digitally "scrambling" a message using a secret key or keys.

CUTCPIP: Acronym for the Clarkson University version of the TCP/IP software developed by NCSA, used on IBM PCs running DOS.

Cyber: *Loosely,* a prefix referring to anything related to computers or networking. *Note 1:* For example, a "cyber cafe" is a coffee shop that offers computer terminals for customers to browse the Internet while sipping coffee, and a "cybersleuth" is an investigator who researches and attempts to solve or find the cause of, unusual Internet occurrences. *Note 2:* While "cyber" is listed herein as colloquial, its use has become ubiquitous and it is rapidly becoming accepted as formal language.

Cybernaut: 1. One who uses the Internet. **2.** *Synonym* **Web surfer.**

Cyberspace: The impression of space and community formed by computers, computer networks, and their users; the virtual "world" that Internet users inhabit when they are online.

Cyberspace: the Internet/ electronic/ digital environment.

Cybersquatting: The practice of registering Internet domain names--usually based on prominent trade names, trademarks, or corporate names-- before the legitimate holders of same have had an opportunity or interest in registering the domain names for themselves. *Note:* Cybersquatters engage(d) in this practice, which has now been ruled illegal, for the purpose of (a) denying the domain name (s) to, or (b) attempting to profit by selling them (possibly at an exorbitant price) to, the holder of the of the trademark, *etc.*

Data management: The control of data handling operations--such as acquisition, analysis, translation, coding, storage, retrieval, and distribution of data--but not necessarily the generation and use of data.

Data: Representation of facts, concepts, or instructions in a formalized manner suitable for communication, interpretation, or processing by humans or by automatic means. Any representations such as characters or analog quantities to which meaning is or might be assigned.

Database: 1. A set of data that is required for a specific purpose or is fundamental to a system, project, enterprise, or business. *Note:* A database may consist of one or more data banks and be geographically distributed among several repositories. **2.** A formally structured collection of data. *Note:* In automated information systems, the database is manipulated using a database management system.

DEC: Acronym for Digital Equipment Corporation, the manufacturer of ALL-IN-1 software and of the VAX or AXP hardware it runs on. DEC is being merged with Compaq, who bought it in 1998.

Dedicated service: In a communications system, a specified set of functions provided to designated users. *Note:* Dedicated service is usually specified in a communications format, such as voice, digital data, facsimile, or video.

Desktop publishing: The use of computers and associated application software to compose, lay out, model, and develop prototypes of documents that are usually intended to be produced and distributed in some non-interactive medium, usually paper, but including film or other multimedia formats. *Note:* Unlike electronic publishing, desktop publishing almost always results in some form of hard copy.

Desktop video: The application of nondedicated personal computers to the performance of video auditioning (viewing) or editing. *Note:* For desktop video teleconferencing, *see* **video teleconference.**

Device: any electronic gadget with an ability to receive input (via a keyboard, or voice) or give output (via screen, or voice, etc.)

Dial-up: To connect to a computer by calling it up on the telephone, using a modem at each end of the telephone circuit.

Dial-Up Access: Dial-Up Access allows you to connect to the Internet from a computer at home or any other place where you have access to a telephone. In order to use Dial-Up Access you must have a modem connected to your telephone line. Dial-Up Access to the Internet is slower than direct access.

Digital: the representation of data by the bits and bytes of binary code. Vinyl records and cassette music tapes carry analogue media.

Digital access line: An access line composed of digital facilities, containing no analog sections, and having a digital interface at the local digital exchange office (DEO) and a digital interface at the end-user voice terminal, voiceband data terminal, PBX or interconnecting network.

Digital data service (DDS): A generic description for synchronous digital transmission operating up to 64 kb/s.

Digital data system (DDS): A synchronous system providing for full-duplex, end-to-end transmission of digital data at the subrate data channel rates of 2.4, 4.8, 9.6, 19.2, 56 and 64 kb/s rates on dedicated private line and multipoint circuits.

Digital Divide: a term used to reflect the technological gap between countries that have fully exploited ICT and those that have not. The digital divide is often associated with the resulting gap in terms of economic development.

Digital Signature: Digital codes that can be attached to an electronically sent message to uniquely identify the sender.

DNS: Acronym for Domain Name Server, a system that keeps track of the names and numerical IP addresses of all the computers on its part of the Internet.

Domain: A domain is the next to largest group in an Internet address. (The largest is the network, or top-level domain; there are seven of those in the U.S., and at least one for every other country.) Most institutions, such as Ohio University, have their own domain. Each domain may contain many sub-domains. Sub-domains are often departmental LANs or "sub-nets"; for example, "helios.phy.ohiou.edu" and "bigbird.cs.ohiou.edu" are systems operated by the Physics and Computer Science departments, respectively.

Domain name server (DNS): 1. A server within the Internet network that performs translation between fully qualified domain names and IP addresses according to the domain name system. [2382-pt.35] **2.** A server that retains the addresses and routing information for TCP/IPLAN users.

Domain name service (DNS): A service to map fully qualified domain names to IP addresses and vice versa.

Domain name system (DNS): 1. The set of databases that performs the correspondence between an IP address and the fully qualified domain name. In other words, the technical administration and allocation of domain names. *Note:* The domain name system contains a kind of naming tree for IP addresses, hosts, and domains, identifying each Internet node unambiguously. [2382-pt.35] **2.** The online distributed database system that (a) is used to map human-readable addresses into Internet Protocol (IP) addresses, (b) has servers throughout the Internet to implement hierarchical addressing that allows a site administrator to assign machine names and addresses, (c) supports separate mappings between mail destinations and IP addresses, and (d) uses domain names that (i) consist of a sequence of names, *i.e.,* labels, separated by periods, *i.e.,* dots, (ii) usually are used to name Internet host computers uniquely, (iii) are hierarchical, and (iv) are processed from right to left, such as the host nic. ddn.mil has a name (nic -- the Network Information Center), a subdomain (ddn -- the Defense Data Network), and a primary domain (mil -- the MILNET).

Domain name: A unique Internet name for a network or computer system, which name consists of a sequence of two or more groups of characters separated by periods; *e.g.,* the "govinst.com" groups of characters in the host name "www.govinst.com", where the ".com" is the first-level domain name (or top-level domain name), and the "govinst" characters represent the second level. *Note:* In the United States, nonprofit organizations are identified (with exceptions) by the suffix ".org", government entities by ".gov", educational institutions by ".edu", commercial organizations are identified by the suffix ".com", and military bodies by ".mil". Outside of the United States, domain names contain an ISO-standard country code suffix to indicate the country of origin of the computer or network.

Domain: 1. The independent variable used to express a function. *Note:* Examples of domains are time, frequency, and space. 2. In distributed networks, all the hardware and software under the control of a specified set of one or more host processors. [From Weik '89] 3. [A] unique context (*e.g.,* access control parameters) in which a program is operating; in effect, the set of objects a subject has the privilege to access.

Download: To transfer a copy of a file residing on a remote computer to a user's computer.

DVD: *Abbreviation for* **digital versatile disk,** *formerly* **digital video disk.** A disk, recorded with optical technology, that contains full-length (2-hour) motion pictures for viewing on a personal computer or on a TV screen (through a set-top box). *Note:* A dvd drive can also be used to access data files on a CD or to play an audio CD-ROM or an audio compact disk. *Also written* **DVD.**

DVI: *Abbreviation for* **digital video interface.** A standard for computer-generated multimedia text and graphics merged in video production.

EBCDIC: Acronym for Extended Binary Coded Decimal Interchange Code; the IBM mainframe internal representation of letters and punctuation by numbers. See also, ASCII.

E-commerce: *Abbreviation for* **electronic commerce.** A way of doing real-time business transactions via telecommunications networks, when the customer and the merchant are in different geographical places. [Mattila] *Note:* Electronic commerce is a broad concept that includes virtual browsing of goods on sale, selection of goods to buy, and payment methods. Electronic commerce operates on a bona fide basis, without prior arrangements between customers and merchants. E-commerce operates via the Internet using all or any combination of technologies designed to exchange data (such as EDI or e-mail), to access data (such as shared databases or electronic bulletin boards), and to capture data (through the use of bar coding and magnetic or optical character readers).

EDI: Electronic Data Interchange - is a de facto standard format for exchanging business data between companies computer application in a standardised form, but usually refers to as proprietary system of delivery.

Electronic Fund Transfer: the electronic movement of money over secure private networks between banks' accounts.

Electronic Money: means of retail payments executed over Internet, which leaves other traditional electronic payments outside of its scope. Alongside with most commonly used smart card the term include:e-cards, trade cards, traditional credit, debit and stored value cards, as well as e-cash, digicash, digiwallet, e-credit, e-loans etc.

Electronic payments system: an array of institutions and mechanisms ensuring the cash flow through electronic communications and timely provision of credit and settlements of debts at much less than traditional system could provide costs.

Electronic publishing (e-publishing): The process of creating messages, distributing them, and reproducing them entirely online, often with a capability for feedback. *Note:* Unlike *desktop publishing,* electronic publishing does not usually generate hardcopy.

E-mail: *also* **e-mail,** and **email,** *Abbreviation for* **electronic mail.** An electronic means for communication in which (a) usually text is transmitted (but sometimes also graphics and/or audio information), (b) operations include sending, storing, processing, and receiving information, (c) users are allowed to communicate under specified conditions, and (d) messages are held in storage until called for by the addressee. Some e-mail software permits the attachment of separate electronic files, *e.g.,* word-processor files, graphics files, audio files.

E-mail address: A character string that identifies, on a network, the point of presence of a user or account, and includes all information needed to direct a communication. An Internet e-mail address includes: (a) a user name that identifies a network account; (b) the channel operator @ (pronounced "at"); and (c) a domain name indicating the server computer. An e-mail address outside the United States also contains a two-letter suffix that identifies the country in which the server is located (*e.g.,* .jp = Japan, .de = Germany, .uk = United Kingdom). An example of the Internet e-mail address format is *john.doe@usagency.gov*. In this example, the addressee is John Doe at some federal agency, which is a government entity.

Emoticon: "Art" form composed of punctuation. Sometimes used in E-mail or usenet news postings to reduce ambiguity or to entertain. Examples include the plain smiley, ":-)", the winking smiley, ";-)", etc. See also Smiley.

Encryption: the coding of data for the purpose of security or privacy.

Ethernet: A high-speed network connection that may use co-axial cable (similar to cable TV wire) or twisted-pair wires (similar to telephone hook-up wire). Data is transmitted at 10 million bits/sec on a standard Ethernet, at 100 million bits/sec on a "fast Ethernet," and at 1,000 million bits/sec on a "gigabit Ethernet." The Ohio University Wide Area Network (WAN) uses ethernet as its primary data path. A standard protocol (IEEE 802.3) for a 10-Mb/s baseband local area network (LAN) bus using carrier-sense multiple access with collision detection (CSMA/CD) as the access method, implemented at the Physical Layer in the ISO Open Systems Interconnection—Reference Model, establishing the physical characteristics of a CSMA/CD network.

EtherTalk: Ethernet wiring used with AppleTalk protocols to connect Macintosh computers and their printers. The same network can be used simultaneously for EtherTalk and TCP/IP ethernet connections. See also, AppleTalk and LocalTalk.

Extranet: a website which links businesses to customers, suppliers, etc. for electronic communications.

E-zine: *Abbreviation for* **electronic magazine.** A periodical publication that is stored on a file server and that may be distributed or accessed via a computer network. [After 2382-pt.35] *Note:* An e-zine that is distributed primarily over the Web is also referred to as a webzine.

FAQ: Acronym for Frequently Asked Question, sometimes encountered in E-mail or usenet news postings. FAQs are routinely posted, typically once a month, together with their answers, in many LISTSERV discussions and usenet news groups. It is a good idea to read a group's FAQ before asking your first question. In many cases you will be able to find a copy in an archive, so that waiting won't be necessary if you have an urgent question.

Favorites: If you use Microsoft Internet Explorer you can save a list of the WWW addresses (URLs) of sites or pages that you frequently visit. This list is called "favorites". (See also **bookmarks** and **hotlist**)

Fiber: Network cabling that uses optical fibers (plastic or glass) to carry information as light instead of as electricity. Fiber-optic cable carries information farther, faster, and more reliably than other types of cable. Fiber-optic cable is much less likely than co-axial or twisted-pair cable to pick up damaging electrical surges, for example from nearby lightning strikes, because the fibers conduct light but **not** electricity. The Ohio University WAN uses fiber for most of the connections between buildings.

File name extension: 1. A suffix that is preceded by a decimal (".") and that is appended to a computer file name.

File protection: 1. The execution of appropriate administrative, technical, or physical means to guard against the unauthorized access to, modification of, or deletion of a file. [After 2382-8] **2.** [The] aggregate of processes and procedures designed to inhibit unauthorized access, contamination, elimination, modification, or destruction of a file or any of its contents.

File security: [A] means by which access to computer files is limited to authorized users only.

File server: 1. A high-capacity disk storage device or a computer that each computer on a network can use or access and retrieve files that can be shared among attached computers. It is a host computer system that stores files and provides them to you as if they were on a hard disk attached to your own computer. **2.** A program, running on a computer, that allows different programs, running on other computers, to access the files of that computer.

File transfer, access, and management (FTAM): An application's service and protocol based on the concept of virtual file store. *Note:* FTAM allows remote access to various levels in a file structure and provides a comprehensive set of file management capabilities.

File transfer: In networking, a service to move a part or the whole of a file's content over a computer network.

File: 1. The largest unit of storage structure that consists of a named collection of all occurrences in a database of records of a particular record type. **2.** A set of related records treated as a unit, for example, in stock control, a file could consist of a set of invoices.

File-oriented applications: Applications concerned with the storage, manipulation, and exchange of information between application processes in the form of files.

Finger: Software (e.g., on OAK or OUVAXA) that gives you information about the users of computer systems. It is especially useful for confirming E-mail addresses.

Firewall: 1. A computer that (a) acts as an interface between two networks (*e.g.,* the Internet and an private network, respectively), and (b) regulates traffic between those networks for the purpose of protecting the internal network from electronic attacks originating from the external network. The firewall is capable of handling the following tasks: (a) isolating internal and external traffic (a bridge service); (b) making internal addresses invisible and directly unaccessible from outside and passing through authorized traffic after proper checking (a proxy service); (c) facilitating protected (encrypted) connections to cooperative parties over public networks (a tunneling service); (d) filtering outgoing traffic for security and network usage rules (filtering or monitoring service); (e) filtering incoming traffic for rogue data (viruses, spam, inappropriate data (filtering), or improper actions (port scanning, overload prevention, *etc.*; (f) blocking forbidden external services or addresses (blocking, "network nanny"-functions); (g) providing log-in services for authorized outside users and simulating the approved outside user as an inside user (proxy, log-in server); (h) caching network traffic (cache service); (i) converting between different network protocols on different protocol levels (bridge when handling lower level protocols, gateway when handling higher level protocols); (j) traffic diverting (*e.g.,* for cost optimizing, accounting, network planning, monitoring); (k)providing consistent, open entry to the internal network (portal service) and facilitating public network address and connection sharing (proxy service). **2.** [A] system designed to defend against unauthorized access to or from a private network. Firewalls can be implemented in both hardware and software, or a combination of both. [INFOSEC-99] *Synonyms* **front-end security filter, proxy.**

Firmware: 1. Software that is embedded in a hardware device that allows reading and executing the software, but does not allow modification, *e.g.,* writing or deleting data by an end user. *Note 1:* An example of firmware is a computer program in a read-only memory (ROM) integrated circuit chip. A hardware configuration is usually used to represent the software. *Note 2:* Another example of firmware is a program embedded in an erasable programmable read-only memory (EPROM) chip, which program may be modified by special external hardware, but not by an application program. **2.** [A] program recorded in permanent or semipermanent computer memory.

Flame: Typically used to describe an abusive E-mail, LISTSERV, or usenet news posting.

Flash card: In computer-based equipment (such as MP3 players, digital cameras, and palm-held computers), a type of memory storage device approximately the size of a matchbook, capable of recording several megabytes of (usually compressed) digitized audio files or data files. *Synonym* **flash memory card.**

Freenet: A system of computer networks (usually funded by individuals or organizations) consisting of community-based bulletin board systems with, *e.g.,* e-mail, information services, interactive communications, and conferencing, and that are available to the user free of charge, or for a small membership fee. Typically provides free Internet access and computer services to people in a limited geographic area, often through public libraries; for example, SEORF (the South Eastern Ohio Regional Freenet).

File Transfer Protocol (FTP): Rules and software that allow computer users to transfer files between computers on the Internet.

FTP mail: A method of accessing and retrieving FTP-based files via e-mail.

FTP: *Abbreviation for* **File Transfer Protocol.** The Transmission Control Protocol / Internet Protocol (TCP/IP) protocol that is (a) a standard high-level protocol for transferring files from one computer to another, (b) usually implemented as an application level program, and (c) uses the Telnet and TCP protocols. *Note:* In conjunction with the proper local software, FTP allows computers connected to the Internet to exchange files, regardless of the computer platform.

FWIW: Acronym for For What It's Worth, sometimes encountered in E-mail or usenet news postings.

Gateway: A network machine that interconnects two networks, which can be similar or dissimilar networks. For many years, City University of New York operated a gateway for E-mail transfer between BITNET and the Internet. See also, Bridge and Router. It allows otherwise incompatible networks to communicate with each other.

gif: (or **.gif**) *Abbreviation for* **graphical interchange format.** A file-name extension indicating a certain digital image file format suitable for efficiently importing image data into computer files or for transmitting or displaying the formatted image on a computer monitor or printing it out.

Gigahertz (GHz): A unit of frequency denoting 10^9 Hz.

Gopher: A menu-based information searching tool for exploring the Internet that allows users to access various types of databases, such as FTP archives and white pages databases. *Note 1:* Gopher is most often used as an Internet browser. *Note 2:* Gopher software uses the client-server model. Type of Internet tool that uses a hierarchical menu structure to organize, search, and deliver information.

Handshaking: 1. In data communications, a sequence of events governed by hardware or software, requiring mutual agreement of the state of the operational modes prior to information exchange. **2.** The process used to establish communications parameters between two stations. *Note:* Handshaking follows the establishment of a circuit between the stations and precedes information transfer. It is used to agree upon such parameters as information transfer rate, alphabet, parity, interrupt procedure, and other protocol features.

Hard copy: In computer graphics and in telecommunications, a permanent reproduction, on any media suitable for direct use by a person, of displayed or transmitted data. *Note 1:* Examples of hard copy include teletypewriter pages, continuous printed tapes, facsimile pages, computer printouts, and radiophoto prints. *Note 2:* Magnetic tapes, diskettes, and nonprinted punched paper tapes are not hard copy.

Hard disk: A flat, circular, rigid plate with a magnetizable surface on one or both sides of which data can be stored. *Note:* A hard disk is distinguished from a diskette by virtue of the fact that it is rigid. Early in the development of computer technology, hard disks, often multiple disks mounted on a common spindle, were interchangeable and removable from their drives, which were separate from the processor chassis. This technology is still in use, especially in conjunction with large mainframe computers, but physically smaller computers use hard disks that are in sealed units, along with their control electronics and read /write heads. The sealed units are usually installed permanently in the same chassis that contains the processor.

Hardware: 1. Physical equipment, the mechanical and electronic parts: the computer, including the memory, keyboard, screen, mouse and printer, as opposed to programs, procedures, rules, and associated documentation. **2.** The generic term dealing with physical items as distinguished from its capability or function such as equipment, tools, implements, instruments, devices, sets, fittings, trimmings, assemblies, subassemblies, components, and parts. The term is often used in regard to the stage of development, as in the passage of a device or component from the design stage into the hardware stage as the finished object. **3.** In data automation, the physical equipment or devices forming a computer and peripheral components.

Hardwire: 1. To connect equipment or components permanently in contrast to using switches, plugs, or connectors. **2.** To wire in fixed logic or read-only storage that cannot be altered by program changes.

Home page: 1. The document that is configured to be displayed first when a Web browser is opened. **2.** The document designed to be the user's point of entry into a Web site, or the page that the user first sees when he or she first visits a company's Web site.

Host: Of computer systems: one that provides services to multiple independent users "simultaneously" through a process also known as "time-sharing," excluding single-user systems like Macintosh or IBM PC. Examples include DEC VAX and AXP systems, IBM mainframes, and Novell servers. Of network devices: a computer used by people as a computer, including multi-user and single-user computer systems, but excluding network infrastructure devices such as routers, bridges, and terminal servers.

Host computer: 1. In a computer network, a computer that provides end users with services such as computation and database access and that usually performs network control functions. *Synonym* **host. 2.** A computer on which is developed software intended to be used on another computer.

Host: Computer connected directly to the Internet that provides services to other local and/or remote computers.

Hosting: the storage and maintenance of the data making up the content of Websites.

Hot swap: In an electronic device, of a subassembly or component therein (*e.g.* circuit card), the act or process of removing and replacing the subassembly or component without first powering down the device. *Note:* Hot swapping of components in devices or environments not designed to support such practice may result in damage to the component or device, or may pose a spark hazard even if the primary power has been removed. And, in some computing devices, hot swapping may not be appropriate because new components may be recognized only during boot-up.

Hotline: A point-to-point communications link in which a call is automatically originated to the preselected destination without any additional action by the user when the end instrument goes off-hook. *Note 1:* Hotlines cannot be used to originate calls other than to preselected destinations. *Note 2:* Various priority services that require dialing are not properly termed "hotlines." *Synonyms* **automatic signaling service, off-hook service.**

Hotlist: A list of frequently used web locations and URLs (Uniform Resource Locators). *Note:* Hotlists may consist of a) lists of bookmarks accessed by a browser or b) lists of URLs at a web site for linking to other relevant web sites. *Synonyms* **favorites, bookmark list, go list, history list.**

HTML (hypertext mark-up language): HTML is used to create documents on the World Wide Web. HTML allows you to make hypertext links from one file to another.

HTTP: Acronym for HyperText Transfer Protocol, the standard way for web browsers to communicate with web servers.

Hyperlink: 1. A software function that (a) is manifest to the user as displayed, selectable words or icons, and (b) allows viewers of an HTML document to navigate thereby to another HTML document or file. **2.** The link created, as in 1. **3.** a reference link that can be made from a point in one web page (traditionally in blue and underlined) to any other point on any web page on the World Wide Web.

Hypermedia: Computer-addressable files that contain pointers for linking to multimedia information. In other words it creates hypertext links to files containing photographs, drawings, audio, video, written text and/or animations. *Note:* The use of hypertext links is known as navigating.

Hypertext: System of linking files (text, graphics, video or sound) through embedded links. Text that contains words or phrases that can be selected in order to retrieve another document. Hypertext is used on the World Wide Web. The system of coding that is used to create or navigate hypermedia in a nonsequential manner.

HYTELNET: Program that creates a hypertext directory for locating libraries, freenets, BBSs and other sites on the Internet that are available via Telnet.

Icon: An icon is a small symbol or picture on the computer screen. Icons usually represent a computer program or a data file.

ICT: Information and Communication Technologies – a generic term used to express the convergence of information of information technology and communications. One prominent example is the Internet.

IMAP: Acronym for Internet Mail Access Protocol, a protocol used between E-mail servers and clients, including PINE, Simeon, Mulberry, and some recent versions of Eudora Pro and Netscape Communicator. Permits the user to organize messages into folders on the disk drive of the server, so that the messages are available from any machine that user has access to. See also POP.

IMHO: Acronym for In My Humble Opinion, sometimes encountered in E-mail or usenet news postings; often self-contradictory!

Information rate: For a frame relay logical connection, the average number of end user bits transferred per second, in one direction, across a user-network interface as measured over an interval of duration $'t'$. The measurement interval $'t'$ is network dependent.

Information superhighway: A 'superhighway' usually means a computer network which can transfer very large amounts of information very quickly. The information that is transferred can be written text, video, audio, still photographs or drawings.

Information technology (IT): Information Technology applies modern technologies to the creation, management and use of information. IT includes video recorders, CD-ROM, telephones, calculators, and electronic cash tills as well as computers. It is the branch of technology devoted to (a) the study and application of data and the processing thereof; *i.e.,* the automatic acquisition, storage, manipulation (including transformation), management, movement, control, display, switching, interchange, transmission or reception of data, and (b) the development and use of the hardware, software, firmware, and procedures associated with this processing.

Information transfer rate: The transfer of digital information between two access points or reference points. Values associated with this attribute are appropriate bit rate (in circuit mode) and throughput rate (in packet mode).

Information transfer: The process of moving messages containing user information from a source to a sink. *Note:* The information transfer rate may or may not be equal to the transmission modulation rate.

Information: 1. Facts, data, or instructions in any medium or form. 2. The meaning that a human assigns to data by means of the known conventions used in their representation.

Information-based economy: refers to a country or region where ICT is used to develop economic foundation and market transactions.

Integrity: reasonable assurance that stored or online data which its intended destination without being modified in any unauthorised manner.

Intellectual Property: comprise two main branches: industrial property, which is chiefly in inventions, trademarks, and industrial designs and appellations origin; and copyright; chiefly in literary, musical, artistic, photographic and audiovisual works.

Interconnection: The connection with each other of the telecommunications networks of different operators so that signals or services are transported over such interconnected networks.

Internet [the]: The Internet is the world's largest computer network. It links more that 32 countries. It provides access to the World Wide Web, on-line databases, file transfer, electronic mail, news and other services. 1. A worldwide interconnection of individual networks a) with an agreement on how to talk to each other, and b) operated by government, industry, academia, and private parties. *Note:* The Internet originally served to interconnect laboratories engaged in government research, and has now been expanded to serve millions of users and a multitude of purposes, such as interpersonal messaging, computer conferences, file transfer, and consulting of files containing documents. 2. The international computer network of both federal and nonfederal interoperable packet switched data networks. (See also **Information superhighway**)

Internet Access Provider (see **Internet Service Provider**): A company that solely provides access to the Internet.

Internet address: In The Internet protocol, the decimal-numeric, fixed-length address that identifies the hosts of data sources, and, specifically, a communication port. *Note:* A single Internet address can have multiple URLs. *Synonyms* **IP address, Internet protocol address.**

Internet Browser: Software package used to view pages on the World Wide Web (including Netscape Navigator, Microsoft Internet Explorer and Mosaic).

Internet protocol (IP) spoofing: 1. The creation of IP packets with counterfeit (spoofed) IP source addresses. **2.** A method of attack used by network intruders to defeat network security measures such as authentication based on IP addresses. *Note 1:* An attack using IP spoofing may lead to unauthorized user access, and possibly root access, on the targeted system. *Note 2:* A packet-filtering-router firewall may not provide adequate protection against IP spoofing attacks. It is possible to route packets through this type of firewall if the router is not configured to filter incoming packets having source addresses on the local domain. *Note 3:* IP spoofing is possible even if no reply packets can reach the attacker. *Note 4:* A method for preventing IP spoofing problems is to install a filtering router that does not allow incoming packets to have a source address different from the local domain. In addition, outgoing packets should not be allowed to contain a source address different from the local domain, in order to prevent an IP spoofing attack from originating from the local network.

Internet protocol (IP): A DOD standard protocol designed for use in interconnected systems of packet-switched computer communication networks. *Note:* The internet protocol provides for transmitting blocks of data called *datagrams* from sources to destinations, where sources and destinations are hosts identified by fixed-length addresses. The internet protocol also provides for fragmentation and reassembly of long datagrams, if necessary, for transmission through small-packet networks.

Internet relay chat (IRC) Internet users anywhere in the world can 'chat' to each other by sending text messages via IRC. Internet relay chat is "real-time" communication, so users must be logged in to the Internet at the same time.

Internet resource: Within the Internet, an accessible facility or entity that contains information or provides data-processing capabilities. *Note:* An example of an Internet resource is a Web server.

Internet Service Provider (ISP): An Internet service provider is an organisation or company which has a direct connection to the Internet, and provides other users with connections and other online services (eg AOL).

internet: Any interconnection among or between private, industrial or governmental computer (digital communication) networks. *Note:* The term internet (spelled with a lower case "i") is distinguished from the Internet (spelled with the "I" capitalized). "The Internet" refers to a specific, historic, ubiquitous worldwide digital worldwide digital communications network. It is the Worldwide collection of networks communicating through common languages and protocols. Also the basic infrastructure for the new economy over which information can be transferred, transactions made and work done.

Internetworking: The process of interconnecting two or more individual networks to facilitate communications among their respective nodes. *Note:* The interconnected networks may be different types. Each network is distinct, with its own addresses, internal protocols, access methods, and administration.

Intranet: Any private network that uses some or all of the protocols of The Internet. *Note:* In an intranet, nodes interact in a client-server relationship, nodes are identified by using Internet protocol (IP) addresses, and files are identified by universal resource locators (URLs). The data being exchanged are typically formatted using the HTML language, and is controlled and displayed using a browser. The intranet may be connected to The Internet via firewalls, or it may be totally separate.

Intranets: using the same Internet technology, but hosted by private servers not accessible by the public over the Internet. Companies are using Intranets to facilitate their internal knowledge management, communication, collaboration on projects, HR functions, etc.

IP address: Acronym for Internet Protocol Address. A device's or resource's numerical address as expressed in the format specified in the Internet Protocol. Each host on the Internet is assigned a unique address number (e.g., "132.235.8.1"). Most hosts also have a name (e.g., "OAK.CATS.OHIOU.EDU"). See also, DNS. *Note 1:* In the current addressing format, IP version 4 (IPv4), an IP address is a 32-bit sequence divided into four groups of decimal numbers separated by periods ("dots"), commonly referred to as "dotted decimals." The IP address of a device is made up of two parts: the number of the network to which it is connected, and a sequence representing the specific device within that network. An IP address may be used on private intranets, as well as The Internet. *Note 2:* Due to inefficiencies that have arisen in address assignment, available IPv4 addresses are nearly exhausted. A newer version of IP addressing (IP version 6, consisting of a 128-bit numerical sequence) is currently being developed. *Synonyms* **Internet address, IP number.**

IRC: Acronym for Internet Relay Chat, software that facilitates multi-way on-screen conversations. Available on OAK. See also, Relay.

ISP: *Abbreviation for* **Internet service provider.** A company or organization that provides connections to the Internet to companies or individuals via dial-up, ISDN, T1, or other connection.

JANET (Joint Academic NETwork): JANET is a communications network which links universities and other tertiary education institutions in the UK. JANET is a component network of the Internet. SuperJANET is a new, better version of JANET which will carry video and audio as well as text.

Java: A computer programming language invented by Sun Computers that is often used for Web-based applications. The program is executed on the browsing machine, unlike CGI, which is executed on the server. This means that as the number of users increases, there is not an overwhelming increase in the load on the server. Java programs are executed by an **interpreter**, rather than being pre-compiled into machine language instructions. This permits Java programs to execute correctly on many different browser platforms, but does slow down program execution. Java programs can access and modify files on the browser machine's hard disk.

Java applet: A small application-program component that typically executes in a client's Web browser, but can execute in a variety of other simple applications or devices; Java applets support the applet programming model and may be downloaded through the Internet via a Web site and run directly on a remote computer; Java applets are often used to create Web page effects.

JavaBean: A portable, platform-independent, reusable component model that conforms to specification defining how Java objects interact.

Java^{TM}: A trademarked set of programming language technologies for creating and safely running software programs in both stand-alone and networked environments. Most graphics-based Web browsers can recognize and run Java codes.

Joy stick: In computer graphics, a lever (with at least two degrees of freedom) that is used as an input unit, normally as a locator.

J-PEG [or JPEG]: *Abbreviation for* **Joint Photographic Experts Group.**
  1. A standardized, file format for transporting, storing, and/or displaying data representing still images and graphical data such as colour and black-and-white photographs. It was designed by the Joint

Photographics Experts Group. *Note:* Along with .gif, it is one of the most common ways that photos are moved over the Web. **2.** Images compressed with the JPEG format and identified with the .jpg or .jpeg file-name extension. **3.** An international standards group functioning under ISO and IEC developing an international consensus on an image compression algorithm for continuous-tone still color pictures.

JUGHEAD (Jonzy's Universal Gopher Hierarchy Excavation and Display): Software that searches for key words in Gopher menus. JUGHEAD is often used on local Gopher servers.

Keyboard: A computer keyboard contains rows of keys representing letters and numbers. On an English keyboard the first six keys in the top left-hand corner spell QWERTY.

Killer app: *Slang contraction of* **killer application.** A successful and popular software application (often written by a third party), that is generally perceived to be superior in function or that employs the latest and most impressive techniques.

Knowledge-based economy: refers to a country or region where ICT is extensively used to enhance knowledge of society in general so that higher human capital brings further improvement to the economy.

LAN (Local Area Network): High-speed, privately-owned computer network that provides direct data communication covering a limited geographical area, such as an office or a building.

LAN application (software): An application software package specifically designed to operate in a local-area-network environment.

LISTSERV: Software that controls mailing lists for discussion groups. Messages are delivered mixed in with your other E-mail.

Listserv/Listproc/Majordomo: Software used for creating and maintaining electronic mailing lists for discussing specific topics.

Local area network (LAN): A LAN is a system linking computers within a building or within one organization. Computers that are part of a Local Area Network can all share information from a central source.

Local loop: this portion of the telecommunications network physically connects end users to the central office network and generally is dedicated to that particular user.

LocalTalk: Medium-speed network data wiring, slower than ethernet but faster than a serial port, used to connect Macintosh computers (through their Printer Port) to each other and to printers, using the AppleTalk protocols. Routers can connect LocalTalk networks to ethernet LANs. See also AppleTalk and EtherTalk.

Lurk: Although this term sounds evil, it is really a benign practice: observing for a period of time the patterns of use practiced and accepted within a LISTSERV discussion or usenet news group, before actively participating.

Lynx: Character-based (**non**-graphic) browser for the web; available on OAK and OUVAXA. See also Mosaic, and Netscape.

Mail exploder: Part of an e-mail delivery system that allows a message to be automatically and efficiently delivered to a list of addresses, thus implementing mailing lists. *Synonym* **exploder.**

Mail gateway: A computer that connects two or more electronic mail systems (especially dissimilar mail systems on two different networks) and transfers messages between them. *Note:* The mapping and translation can be quite complex, and can require a store-and-forward scheme whereby the message is received from one system completely before it is transmitted to the next system after suitable translations.

Mailing list: Any one of a number of automated e-mail distribution programs that provide a forum for information exchange for professional, educational, and special interest groups. *Note:* Subscribers post messages to the list address and messages are then distributed to all subscribers.

Mainframe: A large computer, usually one to which other computers and/or terminals are connected to share its resources and computing power.

Malicious applets: Small application programs automatically downloaded and executed that perform an unauthorized function on an information system (IS).

Malicious code: Software or firmware capable of performing an unauthorized function on an information system (IS).

Menu Shell: The character cell software on the OAK internet access and E-mail system that provides on-screen prompts and interprets the keys typed by the user.

Modem (MODulator-dEModulator): A modem translates signals so that computer information can be carried over ordinary telephone lines. You will probably need a modem if you want to access the Internet from home.

Modem: *Acronym for* **modulator /demodulator. 1.** In general, a device that both modulates and demodulates signals. It is connected between a computer's serial port and a telephone line to permit the exchange of data with a distant system. **2.** In computer communications, a device used for converting digital signals into, and recovering them from, quasi-analog signals suitable for transmission over analog communications channels. *Note:* Many additional functions may be added to a modem to provide for customer service and control features. *Synonym* **signal conversion equipment. 3.** In FDM carrier systems, a device that converts the voice band to, and recovers it from, the first level of frequency translation.

Monitor: The computer monitor is the screen that is used with a computer. It is also known as a VDU (visual display unit).

Mosaic: Graphical browser for the web; versions exist for IBM PC, Macintosh, and unix workstations. See also, Lynx and Netscape.

Mouse: A mouse is a small plastic box with buttons on top and a rolling ball or optical 'reader' underneath. You move the mouse across a flat surface (such as a mouse mat) to highlight words or objects and move them around the screen. If you want to use the Internet you must have a mouse attached to your computer.

MP3: A standard wave file format (with a ".wav" file extension) for digitally encoded and compresses music files (similar to the format used for CD music files). *Note:* MP3 files can be stored or downloaded from the Web or other media and played on suitable players.

MPEG: MPEG is a way of storing video on computer disk. It was designed by the Moving Photographic Experts Group.

MS-DOS (Microsoft - Disc Operating System): MS-DOS is the operating system for IBM PC-compatible microcomputers. (See Operating system (OS))

Multimedia: an interactive combination of text, graphics, animation, images, audio and video displayed by and under the control of a PC.

Multiprocessing: 1. Simultaneous processing by two or more processors acting in concert. **2.** The simultaneous execution of two or more computer programs or sequences of instructions by a single processor.

Multitasking: The concurrent performance or interleaved execution of two or more tasks. *Synonym* **concurrent operation.**

NCSA: Acronym for National Center for Supercomputing Applications.

Net control station (NCS): 1. A radio station that performs net control functions, such as controlling traffic and enforcing operational discipline. [From Weik '89] **2.** [A] terminal in a secure telecommunications net responsible for distributing key in electronic form to the members of the net.

Netiquette: *[Slang] A contraction of* **network etiquette.** The written or unwritten rules of etiquette that govern online interaction between users on the Internet (observed in varying degrees). *Note:* Some typical rules are a ban on profane or offensive language, a requirement to respect other users, and a ban on floods of unsolicited advertisements. Netiquette rules may be enforced by a moderator or may be self-policed by other users.

Netscape: Graphical browser for the web; versions exist for IBM PC, Macintosh, and unix workstations. Developed recently by many of the same programmers who first developed Mosaic. See also, Lynx and Mosaic.

Network: Hardware and software that facilitates direct communication between computer systems. It is an electronic system which links computers, computer systems and peripherals such as file servers and printers. Sometimes used generically, as in "voice and data networks," to include the telephone system. Peer-to-peer networks, such as the internet, connect computers to each other; terminal networks, such as IBM's original SNA, connect terminals and other peripheral devices to a central computer system.

Network address: The signaling point code, containing for U.S. national networks, the network identification, network cluster, and network cluster member fields (24 bits).

Network architecture: 1. The design principles, physical configuration, functional organization, operational procedures, and data formats used as the bases for the design, construction, modification, and operation of a communications network. **2.** The structure of an existing communications network, including the physical configuration, facilities, operational structure, operational procedures, and the data formats in use.

Network browser: A computer program for browsing hyperlinked documents (especially on the Web). *Note 1:* A network browser formats and displays information so obtained in a form useful to the viewer. *Note 2:* A network browser may function in a graphical mode or in a text-only mode.

Network cluster: The field in the U.S. signaling point code structure that identifies groups of signaling points and individual STPs (signaling transfer points) of a signaling network.

Network connectivity: The topological description of a network that specifies, in terms of circuit termination locations and quantities, the interconnection of the transmission nodes.

Network interface: 1. The point of interconnection between a user terminal and a private or public network. **2.** The point of interconnection between the public switched network and a privately owned terminal. *Note: Code of Federal Regulations,* Title 47, part 68, stipulates the interface parameters. **3.** The point of interconnection between one network and another network. **4.** The point of demarcation between the carrier's facilities and the customer installation, which establishes the technical interface and division of operational responsibility. In this definition, the term "customer" refers to the end-user.

Network management: The execution of the set of functions required for controlling, planning, allocating, deploying, coordinating, and monitoring the resources of a telecommunications network, including performing functions such as initial network planning, frequency allocation, predetermined traffic routing to support load balancing, cryptographic key distribution authorization, configuration management, fault management, security management, performance management, and accounting management. *Note:* Network management does not include user terminal equipment.

Network provider: The organization that maintains and operates the network components required for intelligent network (IN) functionality.

A network provider may also take more than one role, *e.g.,* also acting as service provider.

Network: 1. An interconnection of three or more communicating entities. 2. An interconnection of usually passive electronic components that performs a specific function (which is usually limited in scope), *e.g.,* to simulate a transmission line or to perform a mathematical function such as integration or differentiation. *Note:* A network may be part of a larger circuit.

News server: A server on a network that stores, organizes, and distributes messages for selected newsgroups.

Newsfeed: Information distributed by a computer, *e.g.,* one operated by an Internet service provider that maintains current articles within selected groups.

NEWSRDR: A software program on OUVAXA that displays the usenet news.

Newsreader: A local software application (client program) that provides access by means of which a user may view one or more forums or newsgroups from one or more news servers. *Note:* Most newsreaders format and display information from the server in a form suitable to the user.

Node: Each device on a network is called a node and each node has a unique IP address. Includes hosts, routers, terminal servers, etc.

Novell: Host computer system typically running on IBM PC-compatible hardware, providing file and print sharing services to personal computers. Novell clients and servers communicate through the network using IPX and SPX protocols, not TCP/IP.

OAK: The host system that provides E-mail and internet access to all Ohio University students and employees. The name is not an acronym; the previous, small, prototype system was called ACORN.

OARnet: Acronym for Ohio Academic Research Network, the regional network that provides Ohio University with its connection to OhioLINK, to the rest of the state, and also to the internet.

Object oriented: 1. Pertaining to, or characteristic of, a computer program consisting of (a) many relatively small, simple programs (subroutines), and (b) one monitor program, the function of which is to coordinate the exchange of data among the subroutines. *Note:* Subroutines designed under this concept may be stored in object libraries, and used by other computer programmers with similar functional requirements. **2.** Pertaining to, or characteristic of, data to be processed by object-oriented programs. *Note 1:* Each data object in an object-oriented program may have multiple attributes associated with it. For example, if a data object were defined as a person, several appropriate attributes might be the person's birth date, social security number, and eye color. *Note 2:* The data and its attributes are considered as one object as they pass between subroutines. *Note 3:* Objects with similar attributes are considered as a particular class of objects. For example, "people" would be one class of objects and "automobiles" could be another, because the objects in the "automobiles" class are likely to have a completely different set of attributes associated with them.

Object: 1. In image processing, a sub-region of an image that is perceived as a single entity. *Note:* An image can contain more than one object. **2.** In facsimile systems, the image, the likeness of which is to be transmitted. **3.** [A] Passive entity containing or receiving information. Access to an object implies access to the information it contains.

OhioLINK: A statewide network of libraries, primarily academic. The Central site includes a union catalog that contains information about the combined holdings of the member libraries. Individual library catalogs also can be searched. OhioLINK also provides several databases (ABI/Inform, Newspaper Abstracts, Periodical Abstracts, etc.) plus access to gopher and other Internet services.

Operating system (OS): An operating system is a piece of software which controls the computer system. Not all computers use the same operating system.

OTOH: Acronym for On The Other Hand, sometimes encountered in E-mail or usenet news postings.

OUVAXA: The host system that provides E-mail and internet access to all Ohio University employees, and to some graduate and teaching assistants. See also ALL-IN-1, Lynx, NEWSRDR.

Palm-top: A small (pocket-size), hand-held computer, often including network-access software, personal-schedule software, and a basic word processor.

Parallel computer: A computer that has multiple arithmetic units or logic units that are used to accomplish parallel operations or parallel processing.

Parallel processing: Pertaining to the concurrent or simultaneous execution of two or more processes in a single unit.

Password history: With respect to a given information system (IS) asset, a log of expired passwords, used primarily for automatic comparison with proposed new passwords. A password history is used to ensure that proposed new passwords were not used in the recent past, if ever, in connection with the IS asset in question. A password history may be limited to only a prescribed number of expired passwords (the usual case) with any overflow (*i.e.*, the earliest) being discarded as new ones are added; or it may retain expired passwords only for a prescribed period of time; or both. A password history represents a tool that may be used to ensure that passwords are not repeated within a period of time that is deemed consistent with the sensitivity of the protected information system asset.

Password: 1. [A] Protected/private alphanumeric string used to authenticate an identity or to authorize access to data. [INFOSEC-99] **2.** In data communications, a word, character, or combination thereof, that permits access to otherwise inaccessible data, information, or facilities.

Patch: 1. To connect circuits together temporarily. *Note:* In communications, patches may be made by means of a cord, *i.e.,* a cable, known as a "patch cord." In automated systems, patches may be made electronically. 2. In a computer program, one or more statements inserted to circumvent a problem or to alter temporarily or permanently a usually limited aspect or characteristic of the functioning of the program, *e.g.,* to customize the program for a particular application or environment.

Path: The portion of a complete disk file name (for example, in a URL) that specifies the sequence of directories and subdirectories within which the file is located.

Permanent Establishment: a fixed place of business through which the business of an enterprise is wholly or partly carried on.

Personal data: is any data, which refers to an identified or identifiable individual, which is not otherwise readily available via a public source(s).

Point of access: A subscriber's entrance to the telecommunications network. A logical view of this point of access has a relationship with the termination point as defined in the generic network model (GNM). In practice, this may be physically represented by a line card connected to the subscriber's access loop. For mobile communication services, where channels are assigned dynamically as the user moves, the point of access is considered to be at the service provider's location. In this case, there is one point of access for each channel and users who are moving use a sequence of different points of access (each one connected to a particular channel).

POP: Acronym for Post Office Protocol, a protocol used between E-mail servers and clients, including Eudora, Netscape, and Internet Explorer.

Permits the user to organize messages into folders on the disk drive of the PC or Macintosh the client software is executing on. See also IMAP.

Port: 1. Of a device or network, a point of access where signals may be inserted or extracted, or where the device or network variables may be observed or measured. **2.** In a communications network, a point at which signals can enter or leave the network en route to or from another network. It is one of the computer's physical input or output connections. The two most common types are serial and parallel ports.

Portal: website which aims to be the starting point though which one enters the Web.

Portrait mode: 1. In facsimile, the mode of scanning lines across the shorter dimension of a rectangular original. *Note:* CCITT Group 1, 2, and 3 facsimile machines use portrait mode. **2.** In computer graphics, the orientation of an image in which the shorter dimension of the image is horizontal. **3.** An orientation of printed text on a page such that the lines of text are perpendicular to the long dimension of the page.

Posting: A message in a computerized messaging system, and which can be retrieved by multiple entities on multiple occasions. *Synonym* **article.**

PPP (Point-to-Point Protocol): One of two methods (see SLIP) for using special software to establish a temporary direct connection to the Internet over regular phone lines.

PPP: Acronym for Point to Point Protocol, software for dial-up network connections that may use TCP/IP for internet access, as well as other protocols, e.g., for Novell server and Apple server access. See also, SLIP.

Protocol: 1. A formal set of conventions governing the format and control of interaction among communicating functional units. Examples include TCP/IP for general network services, SMTP for mail transfer, FTP for file transfer, AppleTalk for communication with Macintosh computers, etc. *Note:* Protocols may govern portions of a network, types of service, or administrative procedures. For example, a data link protocol is the specification of methods whereby data communications over a data link are performed in terms of the particular transmission mode, control procedures, and recovery procedures. **2.** In layered communications system architecture, a formal set of procedures that are adopted to facilitate functional interoperation within the layered hierarchy. **3.** [In INFOSEC, a] set of rules and formats, semantic and syntactic, permitting information systems (IS's) to exchange information.

Public key cryptography: 1. The type of cryptography in which the encryption process is publicly available and unprotected, but in which a part of the decryption key is protected so that only a party with knowledge of both parts of the decryption process can decrypt the cipher text. *Note:* Commonly called non-secret encryption in professional cryptologic circles. FIREFLY is an application of public key cryptography. [NIS] **2.** [An] Encryption system using a linked pair of keys. What one pair of keys encrypts, the other pair decrypts.

Public-key encryption: A form of encryption that utilizes a unique pair of keys, one (the "public key ") being openly known, and the other (the "private key "), being known only to the recipient of an encrypted message. *Note 1:* At the recipient's discretion, the public key is made available to those who may have occasion to send an encrypted message to that recipient. The sender uses the recipient's public key to encrypt a message. The encrypted message, which cannot be decrypted by means of the public key, is then delivered by conventional means to the recipient, who uses the matching private key to decrypt the message. *Note 2:* Public-key encryption can also be used to add a digital signature to publicly posted electronic messages. The poster of an electronic message feeds the text of the message into the encryption program, along with the poster's private key. A unique block of text (the digital signature) is generated and attached to the end of the message. Any other reader of the message can use the poster's public key to analyze the message text and the signature block. The encryption software will indicate whether or not the message text matches the digital signature. *Note 3:* Users of public-key encryption systems may register their public keys in several public databases.

QWERTY keyboard: (See **Keyboard**)

RAM (random access memory): RAM is used to run a program such as a word processing package. RAM can both read and write (record) information.

Raster: A predetermined pattern of scanning lines within a display space. *Note:* An example of a raster is the pattern followed by an electron beam scanning the screen of a television camera or receiver.

Read access: 1. In computer or data processing technology, the privilege (or capability) of reading electronically the information in a file or data base, without the privilege (or capability) to modify it. *Synonym* **read-only access.**

Real time: 1. The actual time during which a physical process occurs. **2.** Pertaining to the performance of a computation during the actual time that the related physical process occurs, in order that results of the computation can be used in guiding the physical process.

Registered jack (RJ): Any of the series of jacks, described in the *Code of Federal Regulations,* Title 47, part 68, used to provide interface to the public telephone network.

Relational database: A database that consists of data in simple tables (*i.e.*, rows and columns) and that has no system dependencies (*e.g.*, pointers to other data).

Relay: Relays allow more than two people to have electronic conversations. It is a form of text teleconferencing. See also, IRC.

Remote access: 1. Pertaining to communication with a data processing facility from a remote location or facility through a data link. **2.** A PABX service feature that allows a user at a remote location to access by telephone PABX features, such as access to wide area telephone service (WATS) lines.

Remote boot: Of a computer, its start or restart from a remote location. *Note:* A remote boot may be accomplished by a hardware or software trigger.

Repudiation: when a customer in a credit card transaction denies having been a party to that transaction.

Restart: The resumption of the execution of a computer program using the data recorded at a checkpoint.

ROM (read only memory): ROM is permanent memory. You cannot alter the contents of ROM, and you do not lose data when you switch off the power.

ROTFLOL: Acronym for Rolling On The Floor Laughing Out Loud, sometimes encountered in E-mail or usenet news postings.

Router: A network device that links two or more segments of the same network. Unlike a bridge, which transfers all data on each connected segment over to the other segment, a router transfers data only if it is addressed to a device on the other segment. This reduces traffic on each segment.

RSCS: Acronym for Remote Spooling Communication Subsystem. See also, BITNET.

Scan: 1. To examine sequentially, part by part. **2.** To examine every reference in every entry in a file routinely as part of a retrieval scheme. **3.** In radar, one complete rotation of the interrogating antenna. **4.** In SONAR, to search 360° or a specific search sector by the use of phased array of transducers. **5.** To sweep, *i.e.,* rotate, a beam about a point or about an axis.

Scanner: 1. In computer graphics, a device that sequentially samples and records digitally the color and intensity of successive elements of an object or image (*e.g.,* a flat, paper object such as a photograph or drawing), for digital storage, transmission, or processing. It enables you to save pictures and text on computer disk. If you use a small hand-held scanner you can roll it across the picture. Larger flatbed scanners work rather like a photocopying machine. *Note:* The collected data are usually stored in one of several computer graphics formats. **2.** In television technology, a device that (a) scans successive frames (images) on motion-picture film, and (b) transcodes the digital data so obtained into an electronic signal (*e.g.,* analog NTSC signal, or other signal, including a digital signal) that conforms to any standard or accepted video format. *Note:* Scanners may also scan video images in non-real-time transcoding. The scanner may provide input to a recorder, to a signal processor, to a transmission channel, or to any other desired peripheral system. **3.** In computer (specifically, word-processing) technology, a device that examines text, *e.g.,* on a printed page, and applies certain character-recognition algorithms or principles to determine the text elements (letters, numerals, and other characters) in sequence and convert them into standard (*e.g.,* ASCII) digital code for storage or further processing. *Note:* This special application of character-recognition technology eliminates laborious manual transcription of text, by keyboard entry, into digital files. **4.** A device that examines a spatial pattern, one part after another, and generates analog or digital signals corresponding to the pattern. *Note:* Scanners are often used in mark sensing, pattern recognition, and character recognition. **5.** A radio receiver that is automatically and rapidly tuned (*i.e.,* sweeps) across a predetermined range of frequencies (band), locking onto any frequency at which a signal is detected. *Note:* A scanner provides a means of monitoring a range of frequencies, and any traffic that may be present, but will usually not permit the simultaneous monitoring of more than one frequency.

Scroll: Scrolling a document means moving it up or down the screen so that all the information it contains is visible.

SCSI: *Acronym for* **small computer system interface.** An intelligent interface device that expands a microprocessor (CPU) bus to facilitate connections to multiple peripherals (*e.g.,* CD-ROM drives, hard drives, or scanners) and exchange data with those peripherals via a separate communications bus. *Note 1:* The original SCSI was capable of supporting up to 7 devices at a data rate of 5 Mb/s over an 8-bit parallel bus. Subsequent SCSI versions feature a parallel communications bus having greater width and speed. *Note 2:* Since SCSI exchanges data with the peripherals over a separate communications bus rather than the processor bus, the CPU can devote the saved processing time to other tasks. *Note 3: Pronounced* "scuzzy."

Search engine (or **Search Tool**): A specialized program that facilitates information (file) retrieval from large segments of the Internet. (Examples include Altavista and Yahoo) *Note 1:* Search engines attempt to help a user locate desired information or resources by seeking matches to user-specified key words. The usual method for finding and isolating this information is to compile and maintain an index of Web resources that can be queried for the key words or concepts entered by the user. The indices are often built from specific resource lists, and may also be created from the output of Web crawlers, wanderers, robots, spiders, or worms. The indices are usually compiled during times of minimum network traffic. *Note 2:* Different engines are appropriate for different kinds of searches, and most can be optimized for specified results.

Serial Port: A medium-speed data connection, such as the Modem Port on a Macintosh or COM Port on a PC, that transfers characters one bit at a time to another device, (e.g., a modem or a terminal server).

Server: A network device that provides service to the network users known as clients by managing shared resources such as storing files and databases and running applications. *Note 1:* The term is often used in the context of a client-server architecture for a local area network (LAN). *Note 2:* Examples are a printer server and a file server.

Shareware: Software available for downloading from public networks and bulletin board systems, usually at little cost. *Note:* At the end of a trial period, users are asked to pay the software developer a small amount for use of the software.

Shopping basket: In electronic commerce (also called "e-commerce "), an application allowing users of a commercial Web site to select products from the screen display as they browse, and then to securely pay for all of those selected products in one secure transaction.

Shrink wrap contracts: Same as click wrap contracts except for the fact that the accept icon is actually a shrinked box containing the actual product or service itself e.g. software. Accepting this type of a contract results in an immediate on-line consumption.

SLIP (Serial Line Internet Protocol): One of two methods (see PPP) for using special software to establish a temporary direct connection to the Internet over regular phone lines.

Smart Card: card containing memory and a microprocessor, that can serve as personal identification, credit card, ATM card, telephone credit card, critical medical information record and as cash for small transactions.

Smiley: "Art" form composed of punctuation. Sometimes used in E-mail or usenet news postings to reduce ambiguity or to entertain. Examples include the plain smiley, ":-)", the winking smiley, ";-)", etc. See also Emoticon.

SMTP: Acronym for Simple Mail Transfer Protocol, the internet protocol that defines how E-mail is transferred between computers.

Software: 1. A set of computer programs, procedures, and associated documentation concerned with the operation of a data processing system; *e.g.*, compilers, library routines, manuals, and circuit diagrams. **2.** Information (generally copyrightable) that may provide instructions for computers; data for documentation; and voice, video, and music for entertainment or education.

Spam: *Slang* **1.** Unwanted or unsolicited e-mail messages or mailing-list or newsgroup postings. **2.** To send an advertisement or solicitation to large numbers of unsolicited recipients, usually via mailing lists or newsgroups.

Spellchecker: The spellchecker in your wordprocessing program scans text on the screen and highlights any word it does not recognise. You can correct, ignore or add the word to the spellchecker dictionary. Spellcheckers are useful, but remember that: they do not recognise a lot of English words that are spelt correctly if you are checking a long document it is easy to make new mistakes by telling the spellchecker to "correct" words that it does not recognise if you spell a word wrongly so that it looks like another English word the spellchecker will not recognise the mistake.

Superencryption: [The] process of encrypting encrypted information. *Note:* [This process] occurs when a message, encrypted off-line, is transmitted over a secured, on-line circuit, or when information encrypted by the originator is multiplexed into a communications trunk, which is then bulk encrypted.

System administration: In computer technology, a set of functions that provides support services, ensures reliable operations, promotes efficient use of the system, and ensures that prescribed service-quality objectives are met. *Synonym* **system management.**

Tag image file format (TIFF): A file format used to store an image using the particular data structure of the file.

Talk: Text telephone: a service that permit two people who are logged in to host computers to engage in a split-screen "conversation," in which what one user types is presented on the top half of both screens while the other user's typing is presented on the bottom half of both screens. Available on OAK.

TCP/IP (Transmission Control Protocol/Internet Protocol): Set of rules that control how information moves among computers on the Internet.

TCP/IP: *Abbreviation for* **Transmission Control Protocol / Internet Protocol.** Two interrelated protocols that are part of the Internet protocol suite. *Note 1:* TCP operates on the OSI Transport Layer and breaks data into packets. IP operates on the OSI Network Layer and routes packets. *Note 2:* TCP/IP was originally developed by the U.S. Department of Defense. *Note 3:* TCP/IP software must be installed on a computer system for it to function as a part of the internet.

TCP: *Abbreviation for* **Transmission Control Protocol.** In the Internet Protocol suite, a standard, connection-oriented, full-duplex, host-to-host protocol used over packet-switched computer communications networks. *Note 1:* TCP corresponds closely to the ISO Open Systems Interconnection--Reference Model (OSI--RM) Layer 4 (Transport Layer). *Note 2:* The OSI--RM uses TP-0 or TP-4 protocols for transmission control.

Teledensity: teledensity refers to the number of telephone lines per 100 people, s rough measure of the ubiquity of the public switched telephone network in a country.

Telnet (Teletype Network): Rules and software that allow computer users to log onto and use other computer systems on the Internet.

Telnet: Software used to logon to a remote computer system for interactive access, in which the local computer emulates a terminal.

Terminal: A device that provides a keyboard and display screen (like a personal computer, but **without** the ability to use general purpose software). Characters typed at the keyboard are transferred to a host computer system, and characters sent from the host system are displayed on the screen.

Terminal Server: A device that connects a high-speed network to multiple serial ports. Provides access to host computers from terminals or from personal computers emulating terminals. See also, WAN port.

Thin client (computing): A server-centric computing model in which the application software, data, and CPU power resides on a network server rather than on the client computer (s). *Note 1:* This computing philosophy allows administrators to purchase one relatively powerful and expensive server and be confident that any external terminal, regardless of its power or sophistication, can run applications on the server. Most "shopping" Web pages, for example, are thin-client applications (*i.e.*, the client needs nothing more than a browser and a connection to the network to be able to search the "shopping" page and to order products). Local area networks can use thin-client modeling to install only one copy of necessary programs onto the main server for many clients on the network to use. *Note 2:* Server software is required to interface clients with the software on the server. *Synonyms* **Internet appliance (computing), Internet box (computing), network computer.**

Thinwire: Coaxial cable used for ethernet connections. So-called because the original ethernet cable had a larger diameter. Thinwire appears very similar to ordinary cable TV wiring. See also, Coax.

Thread: A topic or line of discussion in a LISTSERV or usenet news group. Because of the distributed nature of these communications methods, multiple threads are going at once. One feature of some news reader software is sorting out the articles into threads. This is usually done on the basis of the "Subject" or "Title" the author has given to the article: if it starts out "RE: ", then the rest of the title is taken to be the thread title. In computer conferencing, a set of sequential messages containing closely related information. *Synonyms* **discussion thread, followup.**

TN3270: A version of TELNET software used to logon to IBM Mainframes with full screen access, emulating an IBM 3270 terminal.

Token Ring: An IBM-originated, high-speed, local area network technology, typically somewhat faster than ethernet. Very few Token Ring LANs are installed at Ohio University.

Transparency: 1. The property of an entity that allows another entity to pass thorough it without altering either of the entities. 2. In telecommunications, the property that allows a transmission system or channel to accept, at its input, unmodified user information, and deliver corresponding user information at its output, unchanged in form or information content. *Note:* The user information may be changed internally within the transmission system, but it is restored to its original form prior to the output without the involvement of the user. 3. The quality of a data communications system or device that uses a bit-oriented link protocol that does not depend on the bit sequence structure used by the data source. 4. An image fixed on a clear base by means of a photographic printing, chemical, or other process, especially adaptable for viewing by transmitted light.

Twisted-pair: Wiring for LANs that uses pairs of copper wire that are twisted around each other to allow maximum data flow with minimum cost and interference. See also, Ethernet and Coax.

UNIX: Multitasking, multiuser computer operating system that is run by many computers that are connected to the Internet.

Upload/Download: The process of transferring files between computers. Files are uploaded from your computer to another and downloaded from another computer to your own.

URL (Uniform Resource Locator): The URL of a webpage is its "address" on the World Wide Web. For example, the URL of the CELTE Self-Access Centre is: http://www.warwick.ac.uk/EAP.

USB: Acronym for Universal Serial Bus, a 12 million bits/sec serial port for personal computers to connect keyboards, mice, external floppy or ZIP disk drives, etc.

Usenet: Informal network of computers that allow the posting and reading of messages in newsgroups that focus on specific topics. It is really network news service; similar to an informational bulletin board. See also, BBS.

UTP: Acronym for Unshielded Twisted-Pair, the cheaper and more common form of twisted-pair wiring, used for voice telephone circuits as well as for ethernet circuits.

VAX: General purpose host computer system, such as the original OUVAXA, shared by many users, on which ALL-IN-1 software runs and ALL-IN-1 data is stored. Can also run Web server software.

VDU (visual display unit): (See **Monitor**)

VERONICA (Very Easy Rodent Oriented Netwide Index to Computerized Archives): A menu-based system for searching gopher menus by keyword, so you can more quickly find items. See also, Archie.

Virus: A virus is a program that damages computer files.

VPN: Virtual Private Network - a VPN is a part of the public Internet to which access is controlled by firewalls and secure tunnels to enable private and secure use by authorised users.

WAIS (Wide Area Information Server): A type of server that provides searching access to text-based databases and ranks results based on relevance to the search. Available through gopher, web, or dedicated clients.

Website: pages of information linked to one another by hyperlinks (usually organised around a menu), with the main page (usually including the menu) bearing the domain address. These pages are on a Web server and are accessible from any browser on the World Wide Web.

White Pages: Lists of Internet users that are accessible through the Internet. There are several different kinds of white-pages servers and services.

Whois: A program that looks up information about Internet users, hosts, domains, and networks, searching an electronic white pages.

World Wide Web (also known as the **WWW, W3** or **Web**).: The World Wide Web is a system for moving about the Internet and finding and viewing documents. You can access documents on the World Wide Web by using a Web browser such as Microsoft Internet Explorer or Netscape. The World Wide Web was developed at CERN, Europe's centre for research into particle physics, in Switzerland.

WWW (World Wide Web): Acronym for World-Wide Web, a menu-based system used to find and access different Internet resources. See also, HTML, HTTP, Lynx, Mosaic, and Netscape.

INDEX

A

Academic Research Network, 36
access loop, 38
ACORN, 35
address number, 27
algorithm, 29
Alpha, 3
alphabet, 19
AppleTalk, 2, 14, 30, 39
article, 39, 48
attachment, 2, 13
audio compact disk, 12
audio files, 5, 13, 18
audio information, 13
audio players, 4
audio, 4, 5, 12, 13, 18, 22, 23, 28, 32
authentication, 3, 25
authorship, 7
automated systems, 38
automatic signaling service, 21

B

backup file, 3
backup, 3
bar coding, 13
basic word processor, 37
BBSs (bulletin board systems), 3, 22, 44
bit string, 5
BITNET (Because It's Time Network), 4, 18, 42
bookmark list, 4, 22
bookmarks, 15, 21
bridge, 17, 42
browser platforms, 28

C

cable TV wire, 14
cable TV, 6, 14, 48
calculators, 23
CATV systems, 5
CD-ROM, 12, 23, 43
cell phones, 4
central office network, 30
central processing unit, 7
central processor, 7
channel operator, 14
circuit diagrams, 45
circuits, 7, 38, 50
client-server architecture, 44
co-axial cable, 6, 14
Code of Federal Regulations, 34, 41
coding scheme, 4
coding, 8, 13, 14, 22

Common Gateway Interface (CGI), 6, 28
communication port, 25
communication, 8, 13, 14, 25-27, 29, 33, 38, 41
communications channel, 3, 31
communications networks, 7, 47
communications processor unit, 7
communications system, 7, 9, 40, 49
competitive service provider (CAP), 2
compilers, 45
component network, 28
computer file name, 15
computer files, 16, 19
computer graphics, 4, 6, 19, 28, 39, 42
computer network, 1, 3, 7, 8, 15, 16, 21, 23, 24, 29
computer screen, 22
computers, 6-11, 16, 18, 20, 21, 23, 30, 31, 33, 35, 37, 45-47, 49
COMSEC, 1
concurrent operation, 32
connection-oriented, 47
connectors, 20
contamination, 15
continuous-tone, 29
copyright, 24
corporate names, 8
country code, 5, 12
cryptography, 7, 40
cyber cafe, 8
cybersleuth, 8

D

data banks, 8
data communications, 7, 38, 40
data handling operations, 8
data link, 40, 41
data networks, 25
data stream, 1
data transmission, 3, 5, 6
data wiring, 30
datagrams, 25
demarcation, 34
desktop publishing, 9, 13
dial-up network, 39
dial-up, 27, 39
digital cameras, 18
digital data, 9, 10, 43
Digital Equipment Corporation, 3, 9
digital signals, 31, 43
digital signature, 40
digital versatile disk, 12
digital video disk, 12
digital video interface, 12
direct access, 9
directories, 38
discussion thread, 48
domain name, 8, 11
DOS (Disc Operating System), 7, 32
drawings, 22, 23

E

E-commerce, 12, 45
electronic bulletin boards, 13
electronic cash tills, 23
electronic commerce, 12, 45
Electronic Data Interchange (EDI), 12, 13
electronic magazine, 15
electronic mail, 13, 24, 30
elimination, 15
E-mail, 1, 2, 5, 12-16, 18, 23, 29-31, 35, 37, 38, 42, 45
embedded links, 22
encrypted message, 40
encryption, 40
end-user, 10, 34
erasable programmable read-only memory (EPROM), 17
ethernet cable, 48
ethernet connections, 48
Ethernet, 6, 14, 30, 48-50
EtherTalk, 2, 14, 30

Eudora Pro, 23
Eudora, 23, 38
EXCEL, 2
exchange service, 2
exploder, 30
Extended Binary Coded Decimal Interchange Code, 12
extension, 15, 19, 29, 32
external floppy, 49

F

facsimile, 9, 19, 36, 39
file format, 19, 46
File Transfer Protocol (FTP), 2, 5, 6, 18, 19, 39
file transfer, 2, 16, 24, 39
File transfer, access, and management (FTAM), 16
firewall, 16, 25
firmware, 4, 17, 23, 31
flash memory card, 18
flatbed scanners, 43
followup, 48
freenets, 22
frequency allocation, 34
frequency translation, 31
Frequently Asked Question (FAQ), 15
full screen access, 48
full-duplex, 10, 47

G

Gateway, 4, 18
generic network model (GNM), 38
go list, 22
gopher menus, 29
gopher servers, 29
gopher, 6, 19, 36, 50
graphical interchange format (gif), 19
graphics files, 13
graphics, 12, 13, 22, 28, 32, 43

H

hard disk, 16, 19, 28
hardcopy, 13
hardware, 9, 12, 17, 19, 20, 23, 35, 42
high speed telecommunications network, 3
high-speed network connection, 14
high-speed, 29
history list, 22
host computer system, 3, 16, 47, 50
hosts, 11, 25, 27, 35, 50
host-to-host protocol, 47
hotlist, 15, 21
hyperlinked documents, 34
hyperlinks, 50
hypertext links, 22
HyperText Transfer Protocol (HTTP), 5, 22, 51
hypertext, 5, 22

I

IBM, 2, 4, 7, 12, 20, 32, 33, 35, 48
image compression, 29
incoming traffic, 17
industrial designs and appellations origin, 24
information exchange, 19
information system, 31, 37
informational bulletin board, 49
input unit, 28
Intellectual Property, 24
intelligent network, 34
interactive access, 47
interconnecting, 10, 26
interface, 5, 10, 16, 23, 34, 41, 43, 48
internet access, 1, 31, 35, 37, 39
internet address, 10, 25, 27
internet appliance, 48
internet box, 48
internet browser, 19, 25
Internet Explorer, 38

Internet Mail Access Protocol, 23
Internet Protocol (IP), 10, 11, 25-27, 35, 47
internet protocol address, 25, 27
internet relay chat, 26, 27
internet service provider, 25-27
Internet, vii, 2, 4-14, 16, 18, 19, 21-28, 31, 32, 35, 36, 39, 44, 47, 49-51
interpreter, 28
interrupt procedure, 19
intranets, 27
inventions, 24
IP address, 10, 11, 25, 27, 35
IP packets, 25
IP spoofing, 25
ISO Open Systems, 14

J

Joint Academic NETwork, 27
Joint Photographics Experts Group, 29
Jonzy's Universal Gopher Hierarchy Excavation and Display, 29

K

keyboard, 9, 20, 29, 41, 43, 47, 49
killer application, 29

L

LAN users, 11
libraries, 18, 22, 36
library routines, 45
LISTSERV, 15, 18, 29, 30, 48
Local Area Network (LAN), 4, 10, 29, 30, 48, 49
LocalTalk, 2, 14, 30
Lynx, 30, 32, 33, 37, 51

M

Macintosh computers, 2, 14, 30, 39
Macintosh, 2, 14, 20, 30, 32, 33, 39, 44
mailing lists, 29, 30, 46
Mainframes, 48
manuals, 45
messages, 3, 6, 13, 23, 24, 26, 30, 31, 35, 39, 40, 45, 48, 49
messaging system, 39
mice, 49
Microsoft - Disc Operating System (MS-DOS), 32
Microsoft Internet Explorer, 15, 25, 51
modem, 3, 5, 9, 31, 44
modulator /demodulator, 31
Mosaic, 25, 30, 32, 33, 51
Moving Photographic Experts Group (MPEG), 32
MP3 players, 18
Mulberry, 23
multimedia text, 12
multipoint circuits, 10
multipurpose Internet mail extension (MIME), 2
Multitasking, 32, 49
multiuser, 49

N

National Center for Supercomputing Applications, 32
navigating, 22
Netscape Communicator, 23
Netscape Navigator, 25
Netscape, 23, 25, 30, 32, 33, 38, 51
network cluster member fields, 33
network computer, 48
network planning, 17, 34
network, 1, 3, 4, 7, 10, 11, 14, 16, 18, 20, 21, 23, 25-27, 29, 30, 33-36, 39, 42, 44, 47-49

network-access software, 37
networking, 8, 16
newsgroup postings, 45
node, 11, 35
notebook computers, 4

O

off-hook service, 21
OhioLINK, 36
On The Other Hand (OTOH), 37
online data, 24
online services, 26
operating system, 4, 32, 37, 49
optical fibers, 15
optical technology, 12
OSI Network Layer, 47
OSI Transport Layer, 47

P

packet-switched computer communication networks, 25
pagers, 4
palm-held computers, 18
parity, 19
PBX, 10
PC, 20, 32, 33, 35, 39, 44
peripherals, 33, 43
personal digital assistants, 4
personal-schedule software, 37
photographs, 22, 23, 28
PINE, 23
plugs, 20
point-to-point communications link, 21
Post Office Protocol (POP), 23, 38
printers, 2, 14, 30, 33
privacy, 14
private network, 13, 16, 17, 26
private servers, 27
processing, 7, 8, 13, 23, 26, 32, 36, 37, 41, 43-45
program execution, 28

protocols, vii, 2, 14, 17, 18, 26, 30, 35, 39, 47
public networks, 17, 44
public telephone network, 41

R

radios, 4
raster, 4, 41
read only memory (ROM), 12, 17, 42, 43
read-only access, 41
receiving information, 13, 36
regulatory agencies, 1
remote computer system, 47
remote location, 41, 42
Remote Spooling Communication Subsystem (RSCS), 42
restart, 42
rf technology, 4
robots, 44
Rolling On The Floor Laughing Out Loud (ROTFLOL), 42
router, 4, 19, 21, 35, 42
RSCS protocol, 4

S

scrambling, 7
Search engines, 6, 44
Search Tool, 44
secure transaction, 45
security, 14, 16, 17, 25, 34, 36
sending, 13, 26
Serial Line Internet Protocol, 45
serial port, 30, 31, 49
server access, 39
server, 6, 11, 14-17, 19, 23, 26, 28, 35, 39, 44, 48, 50
signal conversion equipment, 31
signaling network, 34
signaling point code structure, 34
signaling point code, 33, 34
signaling points, 34

signaling, 1, 21, 33, 34
Simeon, 23
Simple Mail Transfer Protocol (SMTP), 45
small computer system interface, 43
smiley, 14, 45
software trigger, 42
software, 1-7, 9, 12, 13, 17-19, 21-23, 27-29, 31, 33, 35, 37, 39, 40, 44, 45, 47, 48, 50
South Eastern Ohio Regional Freenet (SEORF), 18
spellchecker, 46
spiders, 44
still cameras, 4
storing, 13, 28, 32, 44
subdirectories, 38
sub-domains, 10
superhighway, 23, 25
switches, 20
synchronous system, 10
system dependencies, 41
system management, 46

T

T1, 27
technical interface, 34
telecommunications network, 12, 24, 30, 34, 38
teleconferencing, 9, 41
telephone, 9, 14, 23, 31, 33, 41, 45-47, 50
TELNET, 6, 48
terminal networks, 33
terminal servers, 21, 35
text files, 2
thin-client modeling, 48
time-sharing, 20
Top Level Domain, 5
trade names, 8
trademarks, 8, 24
traffic routing, 34
traffic, 1, 16, 32, 34, 42-44

transfer rates, 5
Transmission Control Protocol/Internet Protocol (TCP/IP), 2, 4, 7, 11, 14, 18, 35, 39, 46, 47
transmission nodes, 34

U

unauthorized access, 15, 17
Uniform Resource Locator (URL), 15, 21, 25, 27, 49
Universal Serial Bus (USB), 49
unix workstations, 32, 33
Unshielded Twisted-Pair (UTP), 50
usenet news group, 30, 48
usenet news postings, 1, 5, 14, 15, 18, 23, 37, 42, 45
usenet, 1, 5, 14, 15, 18, 23, 30, 35, 37, 42, 45, 48
user communications, 1
user terminal, 34

V

VAX, 9, 20, 50
VersaTerm, 2
Very Easy Rodent Oriented Netwide Index to Computerized Archives (VERONICA), 2, 50
video auditioning, 9
video production, 12
video recorders, 23
video teleconference, 9
video, 4, 5, 9, 22, 23, 28, 32, 43, 45
Virtual Private Network (VPN), 50
visual display unit (VDU), 31, 50
voice terminal, 10
voice, 5, 9, 31, 33, 45, 50
voiceband data terminal, 10

W

WAN port, 47

wanderers, 44
wave file format, 32
Web browser, 4, 20, 22, 28, 51
Web crawlers, 44
Web pages, 6, 48
Web server, 22, 26
webzine, 15
Wide Area Network (WAN), 14, 15
WordPerfect, 2
wordprocessing program, 46
word-processor files, 13
World Wide Web (WWW), 5, 15, 22, 24, 25, 49-51
worldwide digital communications network, 26
worms, 44
written text, 22, 23
WWW addresses, 15

Z

ZIP disk drives, 49